POWER STEERING

By M. J. SCOTT

Copyright 2016 M. J. Scott, USA

Published by Daniel Wetta Publishing

Other Titles by M. J. Scott:
Journey into Fulfillment
Time On the Turn

Please visit author website at
http://danielwetta.com/author-m-j-scott/

Cover design: Daniel Wetta

Table of Contents: Page

Foreword
Chapter One: Seat Belts, Please
    Hello Power Steering   1
    Destiny   7
    Power Timing and Cruise Control   8
    Power Steering On Sunday   10
    Surprise   20
Chapter Two: Stoplights   23
    Measuring   25
    Heavy   28
    Holiday   29
    A New Beginning   30
    The Ordinary   34
    Where Goes Time?   39
    Who   46
    Aloneness   50
    Glucose Power   52
    Creative Juices Rising   53
    Reaching for Tomorrow   54
    A Melting Name   55
    Unbounded Treasures   56
    Haven   57
    Praise   58

Chapter Three: Lane Changes 59
 Threshold 62
 Readers Beware 63
 Life Views 64
 Emotions Released 67
 Tornado Watch 68
 Pillow Case 70
 Rhythms 71
 Magnetic Direction 72
 Hometown Culture 74
 Power Steering Power 76
 Sharing 77
 Searching for Joy 82
Chapter Four: Welcome Home 85
 A Popular Word: Love 92
 Meandering 96
 Midnight Calling 98
 Power Steering Returns 100
 Eagles of Freedom 105
 Inner Strength 106
 Blessings 108
Acknowledgements 109
About the Author 111

Foreword

Power Steering is a series of vignette-style articles illuminating the power of intuitive feelings and insight, a gift which you too can experience. The meditations in this book will provide mini-moments of surprise and joy. Start to listen to your hidden inner urges and become the architect of your own destiny!

The first visualization is a car with zero power-steering fluid, when this is suddenly an experience of turning off the main road. Super strength of muscles and mind to execute the next turn. So near to home, yet so many turns required! The hope of strength is to say, "Okay Lord just get us home!" It's this asking of faith that precedes each turn and gets us safely home. The empty power steering fluid is replaced, and life seems back to traveling normal. Faith to go again, and several miles are smooth and flowing. But a new leak of fluid when arriving at a new destination suddenly again requires heavy effort and prayer. The multiplication of will power and asking power makes the journey possible. Heavy-duty driving only three miles and returning home, with five major turns. The wheel was obstinate, and the ancient Chevy Cavalier required unseen horses of old-fashioned-strength. Body, mind and spirit were called again. "Okay, Lord just get us home safely!" It was really a test of faith, strength, and strong belief. Ordinary into the extraordinary, and a new book was born and its title!

No more towing, except to know that there's power in prayer. A new lesson learning in going with the flow.

Chapter One: Seat Belts, Please

"Hello, Power Steering!"

Mind's question for the four o'clock hours, all is still dark, "Do I read or write?" The coffee and toast have been the source of raising the sugar level. Now, how should I begin to raise my inner source?

Prepare with all the instruments needed, and put your mind in drive, not reverse. That little nudge of thought that's always just around the corner of mind waves. "Wait and listen – check for the recipe of thankfulness." That's always the ingredient to opening the door of eternal time. No need to anticipate the next moment as it will be right on the tip of thought.

"Thank you Father."

This is a pajama and bathrobe day. No, it's not a sick thing, it's time to finish reading a delightful book, and being grateful has crossed the threshold of my home. To just let the ceiling-fan fill the house with freshness from the open doors. No pretenses of makeup or what to put on. Just letting neutral take center stage. Maybe that's all that needs to be done, to leave business to rest beside the shoes. If you laugh, then this is an acknowledgement of being

1

awake. The joy of expression becomes a new soul friend.

Oh! The air conditioner just came on and jarred this moment. That artificial cooling surrounding…

Stretching out one's hand is a beginning of unregistered thought. It's an automatic extension becoming the brain's initiation. The result can produce an unseen guiding moment of the soul's reach into physical reality. An exciting phenomenon! The creative edge leading and exploring. This could be as simple as reading or writing. Deep thoughts take on unforeseen personalities, unique to each soul resident. This is the miracle of life!

Recorded gems of time can be found in silence. Neither mystical nor ordinary, brought about by the honest surrender of self. No pushing or punishing, just an abandonment into another dimension of living and learning. Time caught in the visible to be shared, or flowing on and lost. Choices seem to have that ability to be exhibited through joy or mistakes.

Steering power again is a prayer outstretched to the Almighty for help! In the midst of night, a smoke detector sends shrilling beeps. No one to make the repair, so self has to climb a ladder and figure out how to turn it off. To dismantle should be easy, and a prayer wave is sent. Push, pull, try to

2

release, and then it comes apart. The night now has quiet and tomorrow isn't far away. "Thank you, Lord."

When the intuitive springs forth from deep wells within, it's time to listen. It's feeling that can't be replicated except through acting out the intuitive expression. This may mean calling a friend, or stopping by somewhere to suddenly recognize being there at the right place and time. To explain this would be individual, but as sensitivity to the intuitive is developed, it's a real source of joy. Recognizing it is like unlocking a special safety deposit box for the wonder of what is inside. It's a valuable discipline of living, just beyond the everyday surface of events.

Temptation comes in many forms, and often so elusive. The age-old-biblical apple has always been around. However, the guise in today's market may be just as colorful.

In walking into a grocery on the edge of town, with a new highway under construction. In many ways we are like the hardworking highway men and women. We too, are always under personality construction.

The beautiful fruit counter was straight ahead, all shiny and welcoming. Maybe apricots will still be on the rack. No, but the lovely fist-size peaches

3

show signs of being interesting. So, in my careful gaze at these straight-from-the-trees-of-Georgia beauties, one stood out. Lifting and feeling its color became a visual delight. Yes, this was the one. No need to put it in a bag, I'll just put it on the top shelf of my cart and move on.

A half hour later, with the check list of needs completed, the checkout counter was the next step. Glad it was a large cart to haul everything to the trunk of the car. Loading completed, and basket replaced at the end of the full stall. The ignition key was put into action and "reverse," the cars direction. Now I see at the end of the shopping carts the peach eyeing me. "Oh, goodness, I missed you!". It had rolled to the bottom of the rack and was just sitting there out of the store confines, and free!

Getting out of the car and rescuing my first choice, all groceries paid for… except pretty Georgia. Thoughts raced, "No one will miss pretty Georgia, and I need to hurry." Drive out, or drive toward a new parking space again? In an instant, thinking, the spirit of truth said, "Take time." Still a choice with the stoplight beckoning. Well, parking again, and this time in a handicapped space, using the new temporary pass from the hindrances of a recent fall.

The automatic door of the store opened quickly, and the original checker had a long line.

4

Little Georgia was resting in my purse, but her beauty had to be recognized as temptation on a Monday after Sunday communion. In a moment, a new check out girl heard me say, "This peach has a story and I've just finished a big shopping, but it was missed in the cart." She blankly looked at my now recovered amusement.

With the shopper's discount it was 96 cents, worth every cent for it to become mine. A week from now it could be forgotten except it has to ripen in its new white plastic bag. It's still pretty, and temptation gets to remain for someone else to experience. Free or paid, it will now be juicy rich and a taste treat to summer. Ordinary, yes, but an exercise as small as honesty leaves a little written joy. "Hello Power Steering."

The breeze of heaven surrounds the canvas of day dressed in azure blue. The morning is like a little hummingbird winging its way toward a nectar waiting. The freshness is shared with a cicada's song, and power steering from above is another gift. A distant twitter of an unknown winged visitor seems as delicate as a flower shadow. This is a blessing of grace to find and share. A voice of a friend calling blends appreciation into the arms of day. High above, a little airplane shares the peaceful sky with directed thoughts.

5

Take the time to trace the veins of a leaf in its etched beauty. It too will soon change into autumn vestige. The hummingbird is hovering in its fly-by, before it will find another seasonal haven. Memories of vivid joys of summer will cloak the mind.

"This space especially for you to record thoughts."

Destiny

When the power steering of destiny grabs
ahold, there's a feeling of fulfillment. Suddenly the
heart and soul feel a powerful wave of love in
residence. The welling of completeness brings
breathless freedom after cages have been ripped
aside. It's that unexpected earthquake that tears
away the old and useless. A revelation of newness
beyond description.

The "ifs" of life have disappeared, and the
timelessness of space can permeate the soul. A fresh
breeze of a new season in discovery. Words flow
boundless through the brain, and the lungs are ready
to burst into song. Even the ordinary of an old dish
cloth finds favor and softness. This is love! The
wind of energy hasn't been drunk, it's that instant of
renewed life with unstoppable peace. Inspiration
fills the power steering well, beyond measure in
potentialities.

Gifts bubbling to be poured out for others to
share. Flights into the heights, in time and space.
And someone once said, "When you take someone
on a mental flight, you must gently return them to
the runway."

Power Timing and Cruise Control

The amazement of perfect timing must be recognized and available to all. It doesn't happen by accident, but it arrives in the sudden unexpected.

A familiar little prayer for guidance will knock on the door of the Lord's well of keeping. When one has fallen and taken a body of severe suffering, it's like getting a handicapped license to hang for help. There's a need for a closer parking place for getting essential groceries. "Lord, just find me a space close to a cart and a place to park." Then the spot described appears and a "Thank you, Lord," is audibly spoken. As this continues to happen, it's like a check list of requests is available.

The cruise control of the car isn't used just for the gas pedal to comply with the posted speed. Then the light changes as smoothly as the little prayer offering, and power timing again brings a breath of understanding.

For an amazing memory to return is having a need for a home in an unfamiliar town and state. While driving along, the author's list began to take shape. A big old house with a cellar, two floors plus an attic, and beautiful windows surrounding. This is the Old South: it requires a front porch, back porch, trees for the girls' swing, and lovely fruit trees. Oh yes, and a water view! Added to the site, wonderful

8

neighbors and a big place to park the 32-foot travel-trailer!

Of course, this was the dreamer's list, but when the first newspaper was searched, the new life was offered. There was the ad, "Lovely Rental close to work and schools." In an instant a phone call was made, and the whole order form of wishes was fulfilled. Oh yes, five wonderful years along the river where crabbing was the neighbor kids' joy. Chicken was offered on occasion on a string. Even the rumble of the heating unit in the cellar didn't deter happiness, nor the sudden surprise in coming down the winding stairway to find a very elderly man standing in the living room.

Whether he had Dementia or Alzheimer's, we didn't know. We escorted him home to his sister's house next door. Locking doors to unexpected visitors seemed to be appropriate. That was power steering and timing during those years of living on the river. This recall now is acknowledging that this force of answered prayer is available, even if it has some outrageous requests. Learning to pray and ask in the specific requires a very delicate balance of waiting and patience. Perhaps the key to thankfulness is knowing this.

9

Power Steering on Sunday

Capturing the illusive intuitive urge feels awesome. The unexpected becomes just a little wavering thought. An emotion often times accompanies this feeling of needing to do something, but what?

A deeper emotion emerges, not always an exhilaration, but in a sense of urgency and a nudge of feeling that the dark side is about to erupt. "Do it Now!"

Who is in need, will I ever see them again? Who is on this very strand and edge of love? A newcomer in the painting of emotion and life?

Okay, so getting to the point, go with this wave that's suddenly reinforced by all green lights on the roadway. In short miles there will be an easy parking space too.

Reach for a grocery cart, exacting weight of the purse, and go in the Exit Door. Apologize to the man exiting and walking only a few steps, a gentleman calls me by name. I stop short. His handsome persona is hidden behind glasses and a cap. On the very edge of his departure, "Wow!" The very delicate edge of time becomes the signature of an intuitive smile. That's not luck, that is a "God Thing."

Sweet grapes of Joy purchased on what is now "Happy Sunday." This is awesome in an uncharted path. Little prayers suddenly being answered. Just moving into the intuitive rhythm, and finding time to look at the deep shades of color and light. The strength in the extended tree roots leaving a spellbound thought of how old and what storms have created?

Stopping, changing camera film, with a hurry to go. Rising – stepping carefully over cracked walkways because of those swelling roots. Stopping to let a truck cross the speed bump, but it waited. There was the neighbor with a smile, "Hello, how are you doing?"

Unplanned timing and the intuitive become a compass. Do we have a new sense of awareness in destiny?

Doing

Doing must be done as a promise made. The night of sleeplessness fades, and the heart of day awakens me. Pulse strong. Sounds of morning are heard on the tracks of a whistle call. May strength endure to fulfill a promise, and ease of rest become a gift. To endure is shallow, but the grace of power will be found. The entrance to that invisible door:

11

"Knock and it shall be opened." Strength to continue on, but not alone. God's grace will be the comfort, and the weariness will recognize, "This too shall pass."

Oh, lead me on, O Lord, today. The door is open to the morning sounds, and my mind is stirring too. The outside world is hurrying through traffic, and the stop signals in the brain are responding too. In these moments the blood pressure becomes normal, and the heart pumps in breathless appreciation. There's inner peace for meditation and understanding. Time to wait for the intuitive to rise from its deep well and flow into being. Breathing provides the required energy to work through the higher potential.

Expression becoming visible is the product of sensitivity. No amount of mounted degrees can guarantee success. The inborn gifts must come to recognition. Dynamic realization that work must be reflected in the tangible. How to do it is another challenging goal. And when? Today? Tomorrow? It's too easy to leave undone!

Time for prayer to seek!

Words

Words in silence rise and, for some, the quick of tongue can so greatly penetrate the sensitive soul.

12

Words can paint pictures for memories, touch, and can even try to emulate the garden of flowers. Study the flowering bushes of summer, and there's physical evidence of the Great Creator. Thought: life is like a collage of words and pictures placed into action. The flow is like a breeze gently smoothing fevered moments. Letting peace surround, and there are no words to explain the depth of grace. An unsung gift to hold as perfect.

Reach

Reach for a higher level of understanding. The stretching becomes the newness of learning.

Discoveries for renewing purpose. New heights to extend vision. Vistas unbroken within reach.

Learning to seek.

Sages of quiet and Quest for the Sages!

Mystical mysteries vented into light. A hand outstretched in welcoming. The awakening of enlightenment. Sharing another breath of blessing.

Is this a time capsule?

Unleashed!

The quiet of time

The quiet of time, untouched by unheralded call. It doesn't rest in the folds of history or

13

common rhetoric. It's a priceless gift waiting to be discovered. There's a presence of power flowing through rivers of wind. Words to describe, search for expression. It can disappear even in an unexpected sound of an ice cube dropping.

Feeding

Feeding the body to inspire the whole being. Purpose of silence to release the hold of stress. The recipe is easy. The preparation is checking the inner energy. No pantry shelf can hold the gifts of the Spirit. The cup is full of blessings, seen and unseen. Waiting in wonder as each holds the key of light and promise. There's timeless moving into awareness. Untouched until released. What joy? What is Love? Gifts Found!

Awakening

Awakening and reaching into the unknown. What is the correct order? Is it, eat cereal first for the physical, and then wait for the Lord's plan? Even this question erases the headache.

Inspiration made tangible can't be hurried: it must be acknowledged, just like the spoonful of cereal. Cereal can become cold. Inspiration can be lost.

14

Learning to walk is taking a first step, then another, then another. Learning to just wait in quiet is just as profound. When the spirit summons, writing can't be lukewarm. It comes from the deep veins of living waters. Truth can penetrate surface, but truth is also delicate and its preservation is a wondrous miracle. Where are we, in understanding all this?

Manuscripts of the Ancients

A new page in destiny, fragile as parchment, and as gentle as fragrance found. Manuscripts of the ancients, transcribed culture, are gems to be treasured. Revealed not in caverns, nor in the lost treasure of sunken ships, but discovered in the unknown energy waiting to be found. The Source of All Light and Knowledge declared by the Holy Spirit. The hand and pen are instruments available for receiving the awesomeness of Great Power.

When the student is ready, "the Teacher will appear!" We are all students in this time and space. Now is so important! There is no grip holding, it can just ebb away.

Rhythm of music.

No words can explain this inner whisper; listen in silence; be ready to reach for new heights, to take a new journey.

15

Just Another Day

It's just another day, until the Master of Thought arrives to prove it is very different.

Brush the crumbs from the clothing and sit quietly listening to the falling, now gentle rain. The breath of life is being renewed and the pollen of spring being cleansed. The miracle of this moment is discovered. The awareness is enough in being received, and released from hidden thought. Don't choke on the elements of simplicity, but fathom the natural process of gifts distributed like stardust. Form a little smile in sharing this mystery for now. Dizzying sounds spell out mystery in the door beyond. Writing can be the sharing of this flow in the stream of life. Return to the temporal and feel the freedom!

Listen! Raindrops slipping to the surface of this planet from celestial heights.

Birds of Wisdom

Mrs. Thrush and baby arrived for breakfast after the storm. Mrs. Dove dropped in as if wearing high heel shoes and a little strut too. Baby-size arrived but left on the wing. The Cardinal call brought the red-headed gentleman to visit a quick beak full. Words unforced, only the nature of life after the thunder, lightning, and a short shower. The Baltimore Oriole is joining the Wrens for a buffet; all is punctuated by a fresh breeze. Nothing is forced by time and words. There is just life in generous white clouds. For me, the Cardinal's call is like freedom from the sounds of everyday life, even from the punctuation of road noise. Just a sip of morning and a sparkle of raindrops in the pine. It's God's touch made visible to view and to enjoy the peace.

Glimpses of discovery. No cataracts to distort the sights. A bird's call to repeat the moment. Shared only with the crystal blue verbena. Little window boxes to nurture. Fragrance of the Spirit, and winging rhythm. The veils of silence blended and gone!

Dawn

A new page as daylight dawns and breaks the night. Feeling this truth is like a breath of spring awakening the soul. To read is learned, but to sense is a gift. Reaching into the infinity as an act of faith and holding to the very garment of spirit is strengthening. The invisible power is a sacred thread woven into being. The grace of peace surrounding this climb becomes the awesome wholeness of promise. A new love offered to all from angels of the Holy One. This ladder of hope to right the wrongs of nature. The spaces between, spell wonder of fulfillment. The gift given, "Peace be with you."

Moments gathered, nourished by love and shared with family and friends. Refreshing as misty rain or a shower unannounced. Joy surfaces into laughter, healthy for growing. Thriving like a silent code of happiness, giving heart nourishment too. A tiny cottonwood seed glides in the breeze with freedom to soar. Moments of delight, while time is marked by drifting shadows.

Answered Prayer

Answered Prayer moves from invisible into visible, and, after the event, it is suddenly recognized as divine intervention. This awesomeness is an introduction to serendipity.

The right place and time can't be calculated; a series of little happenings moves you there. An appointment made on time suddenly becomes *not yet my turn.* Walking through a well-packed room and waiting silently. "It's okay that someone took my appointment time. I'm not in a hurry." Choosing another chair when the whole room was like a stage with the actors being readied for a prom. It's okay!

A new empty seat next to me, the only one available, and a lovely woman sat down. We exchanged a smile and I said, "It's very busy today!" She responded with, "There's so much traffic, and I haven't been out of the house in two weeks." I asked, "What do you do?" With a lovely voice she responded. "*Oh my*, this is serendipity, as you are the person that I needed to find!" We quickly exchanged names, but she was off to her appointment, so her daughter sat down to give me e-mail exchanges and phone numbers. A little later I walked back and told the lovely lady, "It was so nice to meet you."

It's almost a year later, and now I can send her a book that she may enjoy.

E-mail, it's time to respond!

19

Surprise

The day the kitchen faucet blew its little spout.
After that, water spraying everywhere with every
use of the spigot. True, those fresh water droplets
have provided a whole new view. Often were the
days of weathering showers of face and counter! It
was time to take a new approach. A phone call
brought a gentleman of familiar face. The Plumber,
great for fixing household sinks and tubs.

Conversation seemed to explode into little
nuggets, "Did you get a vacation this summer?" "I
sure did we went to Newfoundland." "Did you get
to see any Newfie puppies?" "No, only a statue but
I heard about a book and I'm almost finished with
it." "A book, aha, what is it called?" Before the title
ran out of the faucet assembly, came out the story,
9/11 reality. It's called, "The Day the World Came
to Town," by an author named Tim. As the synopsis
began to unfold, the book just had to be located. My
sharing of a library-return with the plumber also
brought out the revelation of his own inner urgings
to write. That was the unlocked secret that got
prodded into being.

"Well, all you need is pen, paper and a space to
get started," I tell him.

His problem wasn't writers block, only his
inhibition to suddenly emerge as a writer who

20

wields both pen and wrench. But…off to Peru and
Italy he goes, and a new writer has been born.

Hello, Power Steering!

Releasing the Brakes

There's a new joy to permeate our living and
breathing moments when the brakes are released.
It's the flow of effortless moments. Each instant
may be like a surprise gift to self. An
accomplishment that Higher Power wants everyone
to discover.

Everyone is given this gift at birth, but
developing joy is written into the deep genetics of
life. It's that well-hidden desire to create with mind,
heart and hands. The mining of treasures not found
in mountains but in the dreams released through this
creative surge. The finding is beyond written
expression, built, and a knowing has triumphed.

Following Your Passion

Following your Passion is music to the Soul.
That fragile fabric hidden from the world by denial.
The passion transcends life, and discovering this
element of beauty and joy brings indescribable
peace.

21

Power Steering provides the ability to let go and let the Master's Gift be shared with others. The creative spirit wells up in the most unexpected moments. A smile may be the signature of a lifting to new heights. The Soul rests in peace. Someone said, "Passion is great, but it must be applied with effort!" So true! When the hidden talents surface and take on a new dimension of productivity, or through the restless quest for doing, the presence of passion provides abundance when the positive is expressed. The struggle past words of discouragement. which can hide passion for unknown time, is worth the effort. Reaching out, being vulnerable, may include risks, but following your passion is a great reward!

Chapter Two: Stoplights

Power Steering opens a whole new dimension of awareness to the intricate building of an individual:

A rare moment of midnight wakefulness and hunger for substance took the form of a beautiful orange. Its segments were hidden until a rotation of slow-peeling with fingers was completed. The resulting round fruit had a nice shell bearing its shape.

The segments began to unwrap, like a new discovery in life's fruits. We are like a fruit placed in the Garden of Life, and from conception to birth, we finish the proper patterns designed for human kind. Lives are built slowly, and the masterpiece develops into the birth of a new creation. As the years are marked by birthdays, the developing segments build, and the creative personality forms a picture of life, hope, joy and inner-self-discovery. Throughout life, the building blocks continue. All are segments of a whole person designed for greatness.

Perhaps now sleep can begin. Goodnight, before dawn breaks for Palm Sunday.

When the dark forces invade the nighttime of sleep then full combat is required to check that invasion. Try prioritizing the work load ahead, and believe that all in good time accomplishment will be rewarded.

Reach for the backspace key and hit the positive side of feelings. A good aide in the devotional side of time will be that wonderful reinforcement into the positive. That's right, the light turned on for a soul growth of victory.

Measuring

When is blood pressure measured on a meter
and also the glucose count? Is there a measurement
system for strength of the soul? Is there a
progression of high or low, or even a temperature
count?

While questing into these intimate elements, is
there a measure of joy to bring personalities into
fulfillment? The developing of life is fascinating
and our Creator always leaves space for continual
growth. So short, this mystical embrace with peace!

The brain may be the control panel! Rooted in
faith...sown in love.

Blank Pages

A blank page saying nothing...
Beckoning only to be found...
Waiting for its purpose,
like everyone...
A oneness in understanding.
Yet questioning the direction.

Let the movement of the spirit hold onto
instructing. Like a teacher ready to teach a lesson.
Newness is beginning.

25

An old song from inner dwelling sings out, "Breathe on me, breath of life." Already a filling releases the inner emptiness and aloneness disappears. These are the treasured moments of surprise and expression. A new stanza to be begun. A page of friendship opens, yet unwritten. "Thank you, Lord."

Eyelids drawn down. A quiet ease of peace fills the moment. Comprehension becomes the mentor, and wayward thoughts find direction. The inner compass leading, one step at a time:

"Hello, out there…Stars in space!"

Poem

Trees speak of stillness against the morning sky.

A tiny whiff of wind reaches as a branch dances away.

A level beneath, the cousin trees take a sigh of freedom.

There's a unison of movement among the trees and sudden fluttering wings.

The birds had found the sun to bask.

Breezes reach the ground of holy and bring freshness of life to beholding eyes.

26

Oh, a bird flutters and answers the song of the wind.

Suddenly striking melodies of peace.

The quiet of today caught by the pen. Then....

"Thank you, God, for a neighbor child's little harp. Abby is happy too!"

Heavy

Tiny soul invisible to the surrounding world in its spinning motion. Only inner peace recognizes its value, importance and meaning.

Reaching for a Kleenex doesn't respond to this inner-being's cry. Pushing aside the thought, and choice has made a conscious trip.

Hanging on by little threads of energy makes leaning on the Lord for strength imperative.

Holiday

Holiday can come without any calendar reminder. Today is mine!

Sitting quietly reflecting beyond the venetian blinds and feeling the comfort of a big privilege. After a broken shoulder and heavy restrictions, there's a moment of being able to make my own decisions and drive my car again.

Little blades of grass glistening in the sun become little spears of joy. Today is the beginning again of watching for the little things that will build this happy day. Appreciation begins to blossom in the joy of top-shelf placement in the London International Book Fair of *Time On the Turn*.

Happy Day as my writing in first person and publishing with pen name has reached a special moment!

A New Beginning

Silence is deep and sustains the breath of life.
There is peace in the stillness.

Reaching to explain this element is like finding
a treasure. Unspoken words from the inner mind
waiting to be discovered. In this motionless
moment, the grasping to understand holds beauty
and purpose. A tiny grain of gold gleaming in a
stream of truth. This is love!

At a stoplight the illumination became clear
that the companion of silence is patience.

A little while later, at a Starbucks coffee lift, a
lady was sitting nearby, and her shirt carried a
message of hope:

*"Let your faith in God be bigger
than your fears."*

As she was leaving I said, "I like your T-shirt."
She stopped, smiled, and said, "You have a blest
day!"

A shared joy with a stranger, but a stranger for
only a moment! In sharing this little episode with
another lady, she said, "Oh, that gives me goose
bumps."

To share a gift of several books with a dear
friend was the next travel plan. In looking around

the store, he seemed nowhere in sight. Okay, Lord, I'll accept this and move on." Walking nearby was a dear old friend from Colombia. So we chatted and enjoyed these reminiscing moments. Her dear husband is using a walker now, but he will always be remembered as saying, "What can I do to help you today?" My response was always, "Just be you and thank you for caring."

No walk-a-thon needed, the two boxes of raspberries ever waiting to be purchased, but the books still had not reached their destination. So, bravely walking up to a man with his back turned, I said, "Excuse me, I don't mean to interrupt your artistic endeavor." He turned quickly, and there was my friend! The books had reached their hand of welcome. Intuitive never can be truly explained, but the unexpected is always such a miracle of joy.

Openness

Let's try P.S. for power steering, as it is as simple as reaching for a pillow to prop your head.

The genuine openness to life and time seems to melt into the promise of heaven on earth. Guardians of happiness are like a choir singing an anthem of praise. Drift into the mellowness as rhythms flow forth. There is no pushing or shoving for a space.

31

It's a whole new world of consciousness ebbing
from a deeper subconscious source.

Thought takes forms undesigned like, perhaps,
a masterpiece being composed. This inner realm of
peace relaxes the physical body, and fresh new
breathing patterns evolve. No embroidery of this
spirit, just a thread of love woven into existence.

What strength will be required to accelerate?

Is there a mystical bonding, this peace and the
body, like a youth growing up?

Revelation

Thinking in the silence of morning brings
waves of timeless tide. Undesigned until its
revelation dawns. It's not the restless waking or
judgmental reminiscence of the past. It's the wave
of peace moving through the ever present, often
unacknowledged soul. There's a veil of protection
in this new awareness. To ask to explain breaks into
unexplained reply. The building of this is a slow-
motion of life's little time-outs. So little said, with
only the preparedness for a new day.

Just to be is enough for this moment. A solitude
reached after a worn out smoke detector chimed.

The restoration of quiet is a gift received. Just
to watch the changing hues of dogwood leaves

swaying in the breeze. Autumn has arrived and with it a sense of relief. Tiny harvests of joy. Just to be! A passenger in time! Soul of Thanksgiving anytime!

In letting the day flow by, it's like the sun streaming in and out. No expectations measured, just the ebbing tides.

If time becomes a burden, then unburdening must begin. Reach for a pillow of rest and follow the downy softness of sleep.

The Ordinary

Writing time can take place anywhere. Today
the raindrops tap out a soft serenade, and each drop
seems to have its own little signature splash.

Parking early to wait for an appointment can
provide the luxury of watching raindrops instead of
counting seconds. These sounds of peace provide
moments of reflection to search for words to
encourage others to slow down and not accelerate
the day. Raindrops can melt and join ripples of
untouched art on glass. A mosaic of shapes, a
provision without cost.

Intuition

When the intuitive seems to have been lost,
there's a wonderment of how this happened. In the
waiting days, intuition may have been there but
never surfaced through busy awareness.

Today it rejoined events with a stoplight that
wouldn't change, so my direction just turned the
other way. Going home for lunch seemed a better
choice, and then an unexpected phone call brought
an old friend to say, "Let's meet for lunch on
Thursday." This message could have been missed,
but not so. Later I asked if there was anything I
could get while at the store. Just an impulse

34

question, it was the magic of "yes a need!" So I believe the intuitive has a rare personality.

Came the joy of taking springtime pictures. The day so beautiful, and the cloud shapes with a rain storm coming didn't change the joy of happiness. Bouquet of red anniversary roses was the need, met with a special sale of eight for $4.99!

Awareness

Ignition ON…ignition OFF! Here beside a canopy of white wisteria, the floral radiance so short to enjoy. The draping vine against a blue sky dotted in white chiffon clouds. This is an April Sunday, suddenly smiling in sunshine after a rain storm. Fathoming the season of luxurious growth is found in the shade of a tree while enjoying a little picnic too!

To desert this site without even a word of recognition is like missing a grace bestowed silently. Thank you, Lord, for this earthly presence, and again the ignition is turned on. Power Steering has been found again after an absence, and so blest now! Seat belt on!

May the heart of land be as peaceful as the azaleas in full bloom, with a swallowtail resting, fluttering and enjoying the warmth of the day. The

35

springtime of garden glory reassuring the vigilant
new day to be its own picture on display.

Timeliness

A beautiful sky shape caught this eye in
wonderment. It was a perfect heart lying on its side
and resting in the blue. Other fluffy cumulus
couldn't compare to this awesome site. In traffic
and moving on, with the camera nestled on a pillow
beside the driver. The camera was the passenger
and the passing traffic had no time to slow. So a
mile ahead a traffic light might help to find a turn-
around and go chasing back to the lonely heart.
Time and wind changes everything, and now it was
ragged and quickly disappearing. Through a pine
branch and one finger on the shutter button a picture
was taken. Never the same as the lovely pulsing
heart shaped cloud. Was it there to be a reminder to
find a new time and place to settle into life and
love?

In the Still

Sitting in the stillness of 3:00 a.m., there's an
openness to understanding. The plans for the day
seem to be ready to be unveiled. The host of the
night is quiet, waiting too for the intuitive soul

36

speaker to provide direction. This philosophical quest is like an awesome rhythm in the discovery. If you don't understand, then this makes two of us to share in the wonderment. Higher Power is the grantor and provides inner peace. Recognized in the instant of now, it's a gift not even requested. A thankfulness to be recognized in this untouched portion of the day yet to rise. Only a moment before fleeting away! Welcomed, enjoyed, and just a surprise acknowledged.

No food for the table was ordered, and instead a portion of time was received for the inner enlightenment of the soul.

Power Steering is being at the right place and right time with the intuitive in charge.

Now, it would be easy to ignore sharing this morning's little Sunday nudge. In awakening by the alarm for a change, I had this urge to take my new book, *Time On the Turn*, to church for a very frail lady. She had looked ill last Sunday, and when I inquired how she was, she just shook her head, saying, "not good!" Sure enough, she wasn't seated in front of me this morning, and then I knew the book was for her today. Her husband was very appreciative of my thinking of her. When I explained the intuitive power of today, he nodded.

37

Then, after church, I had planned to drive out to the river to write and walk around Jamestown. The early spring sun becoming very warm, and realizing I wasn't properly dressed to be vacation writing. Skirt, blouse, jacket and pretty shoes... oh no, best go home first. The driving home was met with a detour and also exiting church goers, so the hunger pang took charge. Home and so blest, and then an unexpected phone call from family to join them for dinner. All these might have been missed, but intuitive always holds lovely surprises.

WHERE GOES TIME?

Even as the pen strokes the words, time smiles
and continues on.

Why time smiling? It's the heart vibrating and
face reflecting.

Tis early on the clock and later shown in
footsteps.

Lingering thoughts expand the time and has its
own direction.

No pulse can be measured by its input, and its
goodness given.

Thank you Lord for these precious seconds
granted.

Sunday of the Soul!

Joy of Morning Time!

Touching time and feeling time are ways of
discovering a sensitivity to the very essence of
breath meeting time and space. There's a miracle of
awareness that is granted in the inner peace of
being. A special granting of thought, rising from
experience found within.

There's no reaching or straining of physical
self, but stillness is first to respond to this gift of
quiet. No fearsome element in this wholeness
surrounding the very station of life. Acceptance is
the nurturing for growth like a newly planted flower

with potential for beauty. "This creative well has no measurable depth, and the Maker of All allows this to be expressed. "Treasures of life!"

Restoring

You keep teaching me beyond the classroom of confined seating. "WOW!"

The energy is awakening again, leaving behind what others perceive and letting the creative juices power activity. Today I woke on Mother's Day with a genuine plan of the usual Sunday morning ritual. The church schedule a definite, but the body suddenly said, "Wait a minute! What about pushing so hard to achieve again?" Maybe today's achievement doesn't have to be measured by being seen in the same pew?

The love of learning began to reach out and be displayed by the neat stack of devotionals, writing pad, pens and a professional magazine. Each drew me into this sight embrace and granted beginning levels of energy. Even the clouds beyond the window were erased and the sun shone brighter.

The remote lies motionless, and eyeglasses are just inert showmanship, but the gliding pen has found a place to race like the tropical Ana off the coast. Each one of these with power steering for witnessing a purpose. What is mine? After I add the discovery of a Persian kitty in my pile, my purpose spells, "Relaxing."

The menu

The night of time is quiet and requires no hurry. It's as calm as the little resting period just appearing. There's a thought-wonderment as how far it might extend?

Eyelids find closure, and deep breaths may bring the light of creativity. Sometimes emerging as from a cocoon, it takes flight like a butterfly. Or perhaps these motionless moments find a renewed luxury of life. Awareness of this gift drilling down beneath the surface of the visual curtain to find hidden truth. Faith that angels will guide this mission into sharing. A delicate path to follow and power steering to find direction.

Philosophical waves can't be measured; they only glide gently through the seconds of time. Tongues can't master words, but the flowing pen attempts to interpret the amazing patterns given. Is there a purpose for the inner person to find the seeds of hope and peace for a feverish world?

"Thank you God, for bearing this answer."

Just fold your hands, close your eyes, and allow your brain to percolate its own menu.

41

This page isn't going to tell you what is your choice! Experience the joy of letting go of the busy steps of day, and just find precious time to meditate.

May my prayer of healing from the gardening effects of poison ivy be finally achieved. This may sound strange, but it's the little common things that reach new proportions of success. The reaching out beyond self and becoming part of the whole of creation. We're each one a segment vital to the Creator's design: The little hugs and praises to lift the worth of another is all a part of purpose.

Power Steering, you are quite a unique companion in moving forward. To share the personal is the essence of being human.

Enlightenment

To the Power of All Steering, where on this earthly surface are the words to fulfill?

There is wisdom beyond this pen-point that reaches toward mastery. Just waiting for the hidden entrance of the ability to receive knowledge. Learning how to decode past time to understand perfection is a sense almost entirely the purview of the blind.

The wonderment of perfection could easily disappear and never be found. The mind is the great receptacle with enlightened channels ready to be

42

followed. Within this space there is no claustrophobia, and like the astronauts above, there's unending weightless responsibility. Spirit of Soul is like a lighthouse guiding each individual to discover the land.

Returning from this night time voyage of a writer's moment has been like a dream to be interpreted.

Perhaps I have received a gift of forgiveness.

History Lesson

A retreat into the history of times gone by, and first met with a young man moaning and groaning, the utterance indecipherable. He may have been hungry and finally fed like a little bird by his father. His soul had been speaking, but I could only submit a silent prayer of blessing.

The history of our forefathers is still found here at Jamestown, where eagles glide and tall pines stand in unwavering silence.

There's a first storm of the season coming, with the letter "A" for remembering. The silent waiting seems to create an awesome wonder. Glides on eagle wings and seeks for its intent as it drops a luncheon prey without hesitation. A little trickle of breeze is moving the feathering tree tendrils. Seeking the perfect word is caught momentarily

43

with the white shawl flowing across the eagle's shoulders.

School groups assemble. "Stay in line," with teachers counting their eager charges. "All will follow Ms. Peggy, look where we are!" Little mini-lines forming without eager smiles on faces ready to explore. Maybe fourth graders by size, and someone standing on a map calls, "You're in England!"

Eagle shadows soar above this sunlit hamlet, and someone yells, "Are you waiting for Providence?" How strange a name! It's 1:30 p.m. and the tours are strolling by, with butterflies awakening in the springtime. History seems alien to children who are still waiting in line for a gift shop visit. At least they are in the shadows of staying cool and tennis shoes for comfort.

Trust

Don't giggle or laugh, but tonight I'm not going to do anything! I'm going to vegetate like many do and watch a successful television show with problem solving and critical thinking. Just to be holding a key, but not putting it in the ignition! This may sound like a mini-rebellion, but I'm clueless to the value of effort spent and the yields to the reader. It's not a slump in pen-worthiness, but an affirmation needed to keep rolling.

44

Without inspiration, this power steering is out of the vital liquid for movement. A favorite song, "Climb Every Mountain," becomes the roadway of challenge. Have you found challenge to passion interfering with your goal to arrive at the peak of perfection? Since writing joy is my own response to a hurting world, can I share this urge to grow into more than a stationary existence with others?

Perhaps the ripening banana sitting beside me is sending an essence of "here am I" to give energy now. A wonderful pulse of thought shoots right into the hand-held key, and we're off again: Power Steering and Us!

A little television banner across the screen: "Trust the Process."

Wow!

45

Who?

Who are we in physical form? Just a gentle little question probing for deeper understanding. The physical form houses health and well-being through a "God given special endowment." If the present is ruled by the past, often there's a search to explain loneliness.

"Children of God" is the answer to who are we in this world of NOW! It's a hefty answer, but truly a blessing to find always waiting its acknowledgement. Fragile strands woven into this body, and no matter the form of race, gender or creed, we are all one in the sight of our Maker.

In order to create the wholeness of love, the severing of kinship must be stopped. WHO? It's up to each of us to extend the gift of spiritual blessings in thought and deed. There's no ownership required, except in the everyday being of our power steering best!

Questions!

An instant encounter in leaving a shopping mall on Saturday afternoon of Graduation Weekend. A figure in the median, perhaps waiting to cross the street, but the light changed and power steering stopped too.

46

Then in a fraction of a seeing instant, a little crooked torn cardboard sign was written: "Anything will help, and God bless you!"

She was limping with a little back pack attached to her back. She wore glasses, short hair, jeans and blouse. Then the reaction was mine! Reaching for my billfold, as the light and paper were both green, I handed her my little contribution and a voice too, "God Bless."

The race of traffic followed. In the late evening I relived that little scene. Who was this woman, and what was needed to help her? Could she have been a graduate student gathering statistics about what and how people will help, and for what cause? So interesting, as she didn't appear homeless, as she wasn't carrying a big trash bag with all her earthly belongings. Could she have lost her job? Only questions linger about "Anything will help!"

Just Around the Corner

Permeating quiet allowing direction for the day. There are clouds beyond but not filled with doubt, just potential energy to emerge as raindrops to refresh the day.

In my ordinary to do list, there's the car to be washed, after a flying check signature to be deposited. But even that could wait a little longer. A

47

new tropical tablecloth to wash... but that can stay for a later soap and water swish. A tempting catalog has been marked to order a new designer slack suit. All these little temptations are just that.

The cup of breakfast coffee may need a microwave to rewarm, but that's ordinary little nonsense too.

The real joy last evening was meeting dear friends just rounding the corner of a building. They were in a hurry, but they put the hurry aside and broke into smiles and open arms of welcome. That's an indelible moment when the unexpected is injected into life and memory. That's it, the important things of living must not be neglected. That new appreciation is just around the corner.

Wings of time and thought have met. A blessing found.

A big unopened ream of paper waiting!

Did the moment pass by unnoticed, denied significance? A tiny surge of power steering became a sudden welcoming sea of meeting crystal deep blue eyes. It's the little things that create a balancing scale for expressions or growth. Being human is the reason that life is granted, in an instant without turmoil when the soul is born. An intangible element that turns chemistry into a miracle.

48

Eyes of the soul awaken when peace meets peace. Outstretched soul-twining hearts bond eternally. Passports into dedication and love. Never alone even though physical presence is missing. Spirit of earth, sky, and sea seems transparent in this savored moment.

There's no expectation for all to understand. The heaven on earth discovered for an instant. Thank you, Lord, for this grace to have been witnessed.

Aloneness

Take the word and split it into syllables, and you just might find oneness of now! It doesn't have to have emptiness; rather, aloneness can contain a meditation moment.

It's a learning process of understanding self before joining in parallel step with a companion.

When a new contentment begins to form, check the solace and decide how this can return again and again! A living force for energy and joy!

A tiny gossamer spider strand attached to a fragile hemlock branch. Fragile sights that shine forth with the sunlight of afternoon. It's gone now and invisible to the eye as the sun dropped its rays upon another creation.

There's a giant magnolia tree adorned with a satin set of petals. It looks like a white candle aglow. It's May here in my Virginia paradise, and the magnolia-lemony scent requires closeness to detect the fragrance. The magnolia shares the azure blue sky and the white fluffy clouds that build a mental picture of "God is in His Heaven, and all is right with the world." A mighty wish, but one that each of us can help to make a reality. It takes humanity to find grace in the little things. Little bird trills seem to claim this too! Have you heard a little frog calling from the quiet pond nearby?

50

Visualization is a powerful element in listening to all who speak. Sounding messages, like little shadows that create pictures. A book cover leaf is bent, and, with wind in motion, it beckons to be opened. Another author's response from the hidden mind. Cottage magic!

A tiny purple-green butterfly just visited a fern leaf. Dancing in the afternoon sunlight and fragile shadows. Did you share this sight too?

Reader Victorious!

Glucose Power

When the physical energy is under-powering
and the body wants to just put aside the ready-made
plans, there is a need for restoration. Why is there
no physical energy when the spiritual side to
Sunday was ready for going to the House of
Worship?

Check the blood pressure to see if it's in tune to
the rpm of power steering. But there's another
element, also: Check the glucose, and the culprit
measures low-low. Two candy kisses, the milk
chocolate kind: is this fast enough to slow the clock
and make time to get to the Sunday service? These
physical elements can be illusive, and just
succumbing to head on the pillow and letting the
world drift away. It takes mental determination to
reprogram the day's schedule and to take care of the
power train.

No ER or ambulance-running, just make
kitchen efforts for food source, and take a front
porch view of the garden beauty surrounding. The
hidden gifts are in full view while keeping the eyes
open to the Glucose Power effects. Check your
instruments before hitting the accelerator.

Creative Juices Rising

Learning to relax is like being powerless to
receive words given, until the moment when their
voices become inwardly heard.

Perhaps this is the only thought rising, until
heralded by a treetop bird's call. Then the God-
given wings of a blue bird stopping on a little white
railing. Suddenly, the sweet fathoming of a summer
breeze yet untouched by high humidity. Absorbing
nature's gifts brings new life in the search for
inspiration.

Leaf shapes, so many in this little forest garden,
sharing veins of refreshment. High above, a little
private airplane is soaring, and the pilot, too, in
elements of peace.

Have your eyes, ears and heart found these
little voices rising? Take a deep breath of precious
air and claim it for earth's health. Notice a small
bee nursing nectar for substance too! The power of
recognition brings change. Turtle Dove cooing.

"Sabbath Splendor from Power Steering."

53

Reaching for tomorrow

It's as close as the very next minute of today.
The "now" was yesterday's tomorrow, so living it
with gusto adds energy, rather than driving it to a
loss.

Thought-driven emotions hidden can become
the inner expression ready to charge forth. Reaching
provides the open door for faith to emerge, and
openness to bring fresh new growth. As seasons
transition, so does every human being, not by
appearance revealed by mirror, but by the actions of
love extended to others.

In reaching for tomorrow, there's a promise
that carries responsibility. This could be as simple
as arms of encouragement or a thank you for being
you!

A Tribute to Memorial Day!

A melting name

Sitting here in a little forest of quiet except for
the wind in the tree tops echoing. The bamboo
sharing this quiet splendor stands three stories high.
It's a liquid moment when, thinking a precious
name, an unexpected tear begins to trickle forth. It
edges to the brim and follows a little path toward
the lips. Slowly, the tear rests on the lips like a
gentle kiss and followed into a salty little taste bud.

This magic place seems to melt life's busy-
hurry into a restful park-like setting. Could it be that
relaxing has just begun? The melting name found
peace against a skylight, and no storm track was
ever needed. Witnessing distance, place and prayer
brings a wonderful miracle of discovery. A melting
name. Whose?

Dreaming now of mountain mists, or seashore
sunrises, sharing time with a melting name. Perhaps
in the heaven of someday! Power Steering, you pull
emotions into being!

Unbounded Treasures

A desk, a chair, and random choice. I chose this
library space.

In looking around I found I had chosen the "Z"
fiction section. Luck of patterns without any intent,
except a chair with light, table and a view
beckoned, and here I am at "Z". Not the end of the
story, only the beginning of writing flow, and
author's company within the stacks of the library
gifts of mind! There's a free spirit here where
volumes are shelved and time is caught by others to
share.

So fascinating this place, housed on a Colonial
street corner. The myriad of dust jackets with colors
so compelling and titles astounding. If you have
never just sat down in a library with nothing but a
closed briefcase and purse, you'll discover the
wealth of centuries bursting to be rediscovered.
Power Steering, you brought me to this place, and
you must be smiling now!

Traveling with eyes for the unique and
overwhelmed by the silence with book bindings
holding and pages undisturbed. I really came to
revise this book-length manuscript, and yet it's still
tucked securely in the briefcase. There was still
another thought to be shared; namely, to expose the
glory of books in waiting. Launching from "Z!"

Haven

Power Steering and a resting pen, approach time with no place to go, nothing to do! This revelation is sought but often hard to find. Can you find this little haven of your very own? Perhaps a lost golden wrist watch wasn't really needed.

Writing must be fresh, alive and open to new insights. It's an expression being ignited like a firecracker! Writing can't just sit still like collected items on shelves. Emotions can pour forth, and there's no need for an oxygen mask unless the ratings designate.

Power Steering, you can be amazing or frightening, depending on the topic of thought. The clock ticks on, and what new ideas have you discovered?

Praise

Anchored in the very core of life, a vibrating of Higher Power. The Heavenly One signaling all to follow His leading. A Psalm of Praise must be sung by angels above. When the intuitive finds this cord of strength, it provides the energy field to pursue higher purpose. Knowing that each one has been endowed with gifts and that these abilities are ready to grow.

Little inspirations become a compass to follow this magnetic course. Your beating heart is a little drumbeat in rhythm's race toward perfection.

"Thank you, Lord, for the message of Perfect Love."

Chapter Three: Lane Changes

Recognizing the breath of spirit in its relaxing element of understanding. It arrives in an unanticipated moment in time, when openness is like a door without a key. Peace mingles into the unpainted picture, tangible only in its recognition. Little brush strokes from divine intervention. A song, "Breathe on me, breath of life," has been shared. The Creator's touch expressed. Wounds of the past have no scars now in eternal time. Healing is the Gift! "Thank you Father."

When the storm has passed

The storm has passed, and we've been blessed by its rushing on. This moment is marked by quiet of night and the anticipation of a new day joining in song. The touch of softness is echoing in the raindrops. These move the earth in renewing breath. Written and remembered. This hour, God of the Universe, in its beat of hope. Every vibrant moment can be astounding, found or lost in a second. Perhaps no one to find and read, until soul thought is introduced.

59

Tuning of the soul

The fabric of life holds many hues and textures. Experiences shade the moments and memory blends their beauty. Complexities build the rings of growth. Quiet and gentle. An attuning of the Soul in recognition. Thankfulness and prayerful sharing. Purpose of being rising. Another benchmark along the path. Pausing to allow inner light to glow. A new language discovered in written visibility. Interpretation just waiting to be.

Hearing the echoes

No need to hurry the hours of morning, but leave each moment to just belong. To hear the echoes of silence in an enduring present. Waiting for illumination is a timeless opportunity. Words resting, ready for awakening, like an early morning song. There is no need to wrestle with thinking, as its own time will speak. Soaring into the unknown of the past or present or future. Loveliness is the gift of discovery, new and refreshing. Reaching for a cup of forgiveness has its own form of healing.

"Thank you Lord."

Letting go

Letting go, and letting God.
Like the clouds drifting above.
Fluffy movement undisturbed by human touch.
Dipping fingers into the cup of life.
Suddenly, the moment has dissolved. Only a
breath of heaven remains.

Direction of thought is guided into the heart of
beauty. Uncharted and yielding into the mystery of
self. The untold stories with scars surrounding the
seed of hope. Building of strength like a fortress and
guarded by the moments of quiet. Is this the soul
seeking to speak? Blossoming! Perhaps it's a
passion flower awakening in the hues of day.
In a microsecond, a little purple finch flew in
and attached itself to the patio screen. It dropped in
and off as quickly, but it had peered in like a little
micro-second of heaven. The screen is always
before us, but eyes and heart don't always grasp the
Presence.

"Thank you Lord."

Threshold

Silence waiting to be found among the little
crevices, sometimes hidden. A mystery without
adequate description.

Threshold, behold! The soul of now surrounds
the body, time and place. Its gift of spirit found
among the layers of life. It has its own fragile menu
of options in which to choose. It's like sheet
lightning without the announcing thunder. A distant
blend of beauty with new depths of the soul
whispering to move ahead. If you haven't reached
this threshold of awareness yet, that's okay! It's like
a jello mix not yet having reached a mold to see the
shape. Hello to this new threshold of discovery
within reach. Guardians of words with living
instructions, like ancients of old providing truths.

Books bind thoughts, but the books must be
opened for the thoughts to be reached. Absorb the
loveliness that can emerge.

Footsteps on the threshold: a heartbeat in
measure!

"Hello!"

Readers Beware!

Joy in the effort of pausing the reading. Climb into a comfort zone and begin.

Every period on a page is like a stair step toward another writing step.

The commas are our little pauses before continuing on.

Life Views

Lampposts entry with a mockingbird surveying the summer view. Here is an old favorite booth. The soup ladle is posing before pouring into the luncheon bowl.

Walkers, talkers, all gazing at the buffet with crisp salad greens inviting a serving. The steam table holds waiting ladles and little mystery contents. These aren't labeled, and my adventuring spirit isn't ready for open aromas. A gentleman is spooning salads to the point that a twin plate will be needed. Such fun to just observe a little chunk of life, and letting a T-shirt topic breathe back and forth along with the knife and fork. It says, "CAMP OUT!" But this isn't the little southern restaurant style. Business people on lunch break and lively voices blending like the sub-sandwich just ordered. Philly cheese arriving soon. Summer is bursting free, as the crepe myrtle blossoms welcome release from winter's cloak. Window reflections produce activity that seem estranged to the setting.

Pen and paper

I just couldn't sleep until my prayer formed paper words:

64

"DEAR LORD, I know your hand of wisdom waits to be unfolded. In silence, I prepare for my yielding heart to understand."

Physical expression is evidence of encountering the spirit of truth. So much responsibility lies in slowly waiting! Wrongful mental pushing destroys the thread of bestowing love.

Reaching for a pen, and waiting for the inspiring thoughts to rise. So many inhibit their writing because writer's block has taken charge. The crevice of doubt becomes clouded by uncertainty. To climb over this hedge of separating fear overcomes the first obstacle.

The feeling of release brings a relaxing tide of comfort. It's like a quiet shoreline in wait for the next wave. Little grains of sand produce footprints, and writing creates the written gems of human endeavor.

Spirit has been given its own nametag to wear with joy. Electronic devices provide the delivery and visible sharing of acknowledged inspirations.

No one could ask for more than to receive, "You make me happy too!" So rare a gift, this expression! A lifetime lived, and never before given this bounty of a smiling wholeness. Thank you,

65

Lord, for this meaning shared. No strings attached, just to be.

Living on a path of joy, filled with special caring. This is the fruit that Power Steering provides.

Emotions Released

Little tears stream down from reservoirs of soul
in released surprise. No thought to induce this
source of release. It just can happen with no
advanced notice. Why this inner soul speaks brings
a renewal again of wonder. There is no label nor
little road map for Power Steering to proclaim.
There's a blend of closeness being created: intimacy
into the supernatural.

Waiting without words or intent to express. Just
gratitude to our Maker for life yet to be completed.
A destiny untouched by human hands becoming an
architect of hope, faith and love.

The Creator's touch of renewal, and a gift again
to be yours.

Tornado Watch

The prelude to this storm is a feverish call of
several cardinals. Then quiet. Even the oak leaves
sense a motionless moment.

A breeze passes through with the jet stream
above, bringing cooling temperatures. The front-
porch view of nature in its churning of clouds and
their rumbles threatening. Time to exit the full view
of anxious oak leaves and travel to the sun porch for
soothing, rippling fountain exchanging little liquid
sounds. The garden deck is silently waiting. The
resting nesting wren snuggles beneath the pink and
white impatient stems. This time brings silent
prayers for boundless protection from Higher
Power. Bamboo trees, leaning and bending, are the
sentinels of strength.

Small patterns of raindrops visiting the skylight
above, and the piercing rain plummeting down. The
red-colored-wooden deck receiving a fresh coat of
reflecting rain. Thunder is masked by the skylight
sounds. This is not a "Warning," just the Tornado
Watch from inside while daylight ebbs.

Raindrops decreasing, then buckets descend
again like liquid from afar. The bamboo leaves high
above lean and sway, but for today these will
remain rooted in natures' soil of plenty.

Reaching for the lace curtains allowing this vantage provides a comforting security that, "All's well!"

Approaching storm

Another lesson in Power Steering, so different from following intuitive direction. Today I am drawing a blank on what should be on my to-do list. There's a storm approaching. Perhaps this should guide decision.

Off to the post office, but there is only an empty mailbox. Perhaps going to the bank, but black clouds make an ominous impression. However, the distant-white-puffy-horseshoe shapes allow the sun to drop in. With no definite plan, I decide to go home, empty the dishwasher, and drink a cup of coffee. Just as the computer says "Welcome," the phone rings and great opportunities are presented by my Marketing Specialist. All of a sudden, decisions are made, and the video book trailer will go adventuring.

All this could have been missed had I followed my original plans made yesterday for today. A learning lesson to allow Power Steering to shine through. Is there a magnetic current that guides unseen events?

69

Pillow Case

On the mid-of-night, wakefulness has broken
my dream songs. Perhaps the last sound before
sleep had been a musical sermon. The inner soul
receiving inspiration tallied in the cycle of joy. The
intuitive blending accepted as purpose to be shared.
It has no measurable length like a ruler, but an
invisible yearning to flow through veins of
expression. Verbal descriptions of this receiving by
this writer are not enough to express its depth. I am,
at least, an instrument of pen thought.

At times existence is the wonderment of why
me? Why now? Purpose becomes a thread woven
into the soul being. Fragile feelings folded and
protected within an invisible shield set by God. To
this humble servant with bowed head and grateful
heart of soul.

Reaching for the instant, and finding words for
the early day before dawn of light. This is the word
of the Lord, by others found too, and shared on this
roadway of now. Reassurance that hand in hand
with the Lord, the day will be bright. This
continues, the peace of rest still given.

Weaving a shawl of prayers of protection fills
the new day with His presence.

"Lord, invisible love is the shawl of the soul, a
covering of warmth for all."

70

Rhythms

Rhythms play in many forms, and we first think
of the world of music.

Today the rhythm of words is flowing like a
river meandering past a little southern town. It's the
discovery of waking in the middle of night in the
quiet untouched. Taking a step of courage into the
unknown and finding visible helpers providing little
lifelines of service. The beautiful people who
maintain the smooth events. The ripples of
appreciation are still felt, all enriching the
experiences of the positive in word, deed, and
smiles. These are the invisible insurance policies
that become the measure of encouragement.

There is no apathy or complacency in these
hamlets of pure genuineness. Rhythm of peace, and
the only snapping is with the crackle of a carrot
slice, cucumber, or the fork scraping up the last bit
of potato salad. Morsels of rhythm where the heart
of our America keeps the beat of everyday.

The last crumb has been savored of homemade
ham and biscuits. Did you order this taste of
contentment? Please do! Power Steering, you are
the guiding force.

Magnetic Direction

A powerful picture and ascending meaning
from an e-mail joy carried me to the heights of
Sunday.

The lure of a country Sunday brought question
of where is it now?

This key of thought led me into the wonder of
filling the gas tank to just go wandering. Right out
of town, through all the stoplights that shoppers
choose.

The country at last! Will I go North or West?
So the left lane drew me toward an old familiar
restaurant. Squeezing the car into a little space, and
walking up the newly painted steps, I greet the
hostess with the announcement, "Just one please!"
The hostess smiled and so did I. Saying, "You look
so familiar!" She too tried to find a connection, and
"No I'm not the harp player," was my answer.

I asked her name, and the flood of recall came
rushing into prominence. She was just now a retired
teacher, and her name brought my exclamation, "Oh
my Jason!" A former student of years ago, but I
knew her too! I exclaimed that I was just drawn
here today.

Home-style biscuits drenched in sausage gravy
and scrambled eggs. Can you taste the moment

72

filled with breaths of happiness? They own this country-kitchen-restaurant, and what a delight it is!

Two Drummers Restaurant!

Looking for the power in Power Steering isn't a ritual but an exercise of letting fate and destiny weave into this thread of living.

Hometown Culture

Sky clouds scuffling for position to rise or to lower. The sun still holding order with noontime tree shadows of cooling splendor.

Moviegoers are gathering in their summer casual stroll. Some with swinging arms around another, and others with closed backpacks for leaving work behind. Our college town in holiday spirit and vacationers in their relaxing delight.

There's a spring crop of strollers coming in single size, duo, and triplet too. Dads strolling and Moms in their slim trim style. Such a beautiful Sunday tennis shoe parade!

I asked the Lord where should I go this afternoon, and it has turned into a spinach-and-artichoke-quiche window seat. Can you catch this little summer prelude of happy hearts and winsome charm?

A breeze just scooped off a lady's brand new white hat, just as a sweet little hostess carried my tray away. Manners are still in full view for our college set.

Massage mats just hurried by, after their hour of confined moments. The owners didn't seem to have a lighter step or refurbished smiles. Surprise, as a stroller wasn't filled with a wee one, but shopper's packages labeled, "Big Event."

A waiting customer at the bakery counter is shaking his shirt tail to help him make a choice! This delightful bird's eye view of my hamlet is filled with pictorial color. Even the fashion show announced as it took the sidewalk runway for a high heel click. Long skirts, short skirts, shorts shorter and fringe dangling from an oversize blouse. Clean jeans and colorful shirts are being shown by the "boomer crowd."

There's a wave of connectedness taking place out here just beyond a frozen yogurt reach. The motion of life is filled with energy, and Power Steering just has been a non-caloric dessert.

A business man came and sat at the next table, left his briefcase, and walked away. He had looked at me as if to say, "keep an eye out!" Returning he took his laptop out, plugged it in, and placed his ear phone on comfortably. Ready to work. As I packed to leave, I told this stranger in our home town, "Enjoy your afternoon". He returned the smile. My gesture of this place is special. Then it occurred that Rachel Carson wrote *The Silent Spring*, and perhaps we are entering *The Silent Summer*. No one was speaking on my afternoon being in this quiet place.

The silver senior couple sat for two hours enveloped in their reading choices, and not a word spoken. Is this an invisible silence too?

75

Protection

Thinking in the silence of morning brings a
wave of timeless tide. Undesigned until it's
revelation dawns. It's not the restless waking or
judgmental reminisces of the past. The wave of
peace moving through the ever-present, often
unacknowledged soul. There's a veil of protection
in this new awareness. To ask to explain breaks into
unexplained reply. The building of this personal
role is a slow motion of life's little time-outs. So
little said, with only the preparedness for a new day.

"Entering contests challenges us to achieve
recognition or to be vulnerable for rejection. The
opportunities are thirst quenching; however,
fulfillment for the few."
My answer is to smile and to feel the release of
deadlines. To allow the flow of destiny to wind its
spool of events into "Let Freedom Ring!"
Earlier, I placed the cap on my pen twice, and
each time it wouldn't accept this closure. So
strange, the power of thought and praise, and
yielding to a new phase of expression.
"Hello, out there!"

Power steering/ Power sharing

Unfasten your mental seat belts of your
computer chairs. Come along on a mini-vacation
into the luxury of sights and sounds.
Find your favorite memory of excitement and
visual happiness. Let these remnants of life you've
lived return with immeasurable joy. The instant will
be of your own choosing, but it will unharness your
submerged creativity.
Begin to join the ranks of those who have
received valuable time spent as a gift from Higher
Power. Open the window of your mind to the
precious resources you possess.
Find the real inner you that's filled with the
natural non-electronic waves of joy, peace and
salvation of your soul.

Well, power steering can definitely be
serenaded like the cicadas out in the trees.
Nourished like the purple verbena recycled from
flower boxes into a huge container so that the roots
could share more space.
Even the screaming fire engines aren't
penetrating the edge of awareness. Looking high
into the morning sky from this back deck haven,
there is a peaceful stillness. Obeying the intuitive
urge to complete the incomplete becomes another

77

awareness. In this instant there's an inner signal, like a soft breeze welcoming the morning too!

Cloud shapes, filled with fluffy edges, seem reluctant in joining forces to make a complete coverlet. Ordinary events can't be denied, but within there's always potential for the extraordinary.

Joy

Have you ever thought that you are the vehicle through which power steering flows? When this realization breaks into awareness, tremendous energy can be received. Be ready to acknowledge this awesome capture of responsibility and to carry this new excitement. This hidden gift is a refreshing breeze dotted with joy. The word, "joy," pushed aside the written word of "happiness." A signal of the unexpected, and, yes, "*Joy.*"

Keep the pen and paper by your side to share this recorded witness.

Thankfulness…
A blessing of love…
Timeless and strong…
Peaceful, timeless, of enduring strength
Freely given…
Waves of healing…

78

From Heaven's touch…
Formless, boundless
Unleashed by the Holy Spirit.
Sunday…the perfect name
Sabbath for the soul!

Season of quiet,
Suspended between the heat of summer,
And the cooling breezes of Autumn
The Soul can now be heard, a tiny urging to enjoy.
Unclamp the lock of weariness and open a new door to *Happiness!*

No quotes to express – it's just present.
"Toast and grape jam, please!"

Mailbox

Verification of inner promptings is a little known key to unlock perfect timing. Today, rainy and stormy with need for an umbrella as protective canopy to staying reasonably dry. Several trips in and out of the house, car, appointments and not everything quite complete. Watching the storm converge, flooding across the Southwest, and an early touch of winter coming to the far mountains. The mail should be in the mailbox for the

79

Londoners, and all nice and dry. Just let it stay there until morning. Time again to feed the Persian Kittens. Everything is fine, nice and warm in my house, and waiting for the Evening News.

"Why not go and check that mail as it hadn't been delivered at 4:00 p.m.? There's a full gas tank, and traffic shouldn't be too bad."

"No!"

"Ok, *yes*, I'll just hurry and put on the wet shoes, the rain bonnet, and pick up the perched umbrella on the porch."

Keys in hand, and a feeling that this is the right intuitive thing to do.

Down the road a few turns, stoplights, very wet streets, and then, just as a turn was needed to get to the destination, there was the mail truck!

"Wow!"

He turned on the street of my destination, stopped at the neighbors', and then couldn't reach the next mailbox because a car was parked in front of it. So this writer got out and said, "I'll save you from getting wet." He looked very tired, as he had had extra routes today.

"But wait," he said, "I have a box too!"

"Oh! Wonderful! This will save you running up the hill and steps to their front door."

And it was a Priority Box!

Power Steering, you are a companion that can't be ignored even when it seems like just a little thing. Perfect time would have never been recognized if tomorrow had won! It's almost dusk now, and the rain continues. Peaceful raindrops and the mail is safe. Wow!

"Awesome! Thank you, Lord."

Searching for Joy

Do we go searching for joy, or does it come to
us as a gift? Do we wait for its entrance and just let
the time rumble by? The shape of joy: Is it an
elusive feeling, or tangible like arms of welcome?
Could it be an instant wrapped in faith or love? The
unexpected has no boundaries to hold or withhold.
There are no decisive plans, just awareness of its
existence, always. Enough, somewhere in eternal
being. No words can describe this marvelous *joy*.
A train whistles and Soul awakes. "Good
morning to a new day!"
Queen Elizabeth Roses resting in an antique
pitcher, pouring forth for you.

Measuring

The power steering has a dimension of
indescribable strength. How it is measured? Will it
be by its performance and smoothness to the driver?
Thinking of the driver brings unexplained moments
of wonder! Is that the sunshine on the front window
producing a glare? Or is it a distant song being
played for listening ears? How can moments be
described in the void of loneliness when emotion
rises first? Like gas free to move faster or a little bit
of fog left in the memory?

82

What is the purpose of loneliness? Could it be to strip the soul of unnecessary burdens? Questions meant to open windows for receptiveness of understanding. Not an easy recipe for living, but one worth the discovery for added purpose. Could the potential be harnessed within and be released? The heart of an individual is tender and must be cared for with lessening pressures so that measurable happiness can be discovered.

A measure of success!

When power steering jolts us to attention, it's so obvious that it must be answered.

Just the instant of stopping before a wireless phone as it rang with an unfamiliar number but a familiar name. It was our lovely pastor calling to inquire if the emergency room is far behind and my wait too long? She's so thoughtful!

Faith

Faith is like walking on a breeze of fresh air. It can fill the lungs of being and become a dynamic key. Breaking this powerful silence of restful pleasure, fragile and so gentle. The song of a Carolina wren echoed the Sunday into added sunshine happiness.

Allow the clock of time to stop for a moment to soar into the heavens. Schedules become directions,

83

but never the dictators of soul growth. Soul's breath was liberated in birth's miraculous micro-instant. All-powerful in the call of life.

Capture thoughts unwritten of the mind, and allow yourself to dwell or just float away. Joy of recognition and recipient of your gift.

"Thank you, Lord. Rest on the wings of peace. Thirst will return."

Identity

Do we ever discover who we really are in this circle of life?

The ever-developing self from birth becomes a revelation of name, social security number, and the vitae of experience recorded. The natural is all that most people ever recognize as their part of life. Yet, reaching into the supernatural openness is a new course in traveling beyond the walls of the moment.

It's a letting go and allowing the Power of All Life to reveal greater marvels. Great Wonders of the World: Artists, composers, and all striving to produce the masterpiece that allows others to experience through their God-given-gift. I'm going to get the magnifying glass and study the details of a painting to witness this brush with the artist's thought.

Power Steering is a valued friend!

84

Chapter Four: Welcome Home!

Working past the torment of other peoples' thinking, like, "you missed church this morning!" Their unknowing judgement is powerful but not defeating. Awareness of little brushes of Heaven is the nuclear power for soul's productivity. Just to stay on this wave length takes you beyond the line of catching infinity. Power Steering of the Almighty. Are you in the ball game to make a home run? A scent of roses…none here!

Climbing over the mountain of the apparently insurmountable is a major task. The quest for a view above the fog is a power steering course. The climb of faith is knowing that loneliness is not to be a companion. When you reach out, you hear the still-small powerful voice: "I am with you!"

There is no power outage from the Great Creator. Lean into the wavelength of prayer, patience and protection. Have you reached that level of awareness? Let the Soul feel!

Balance

Power Steering, although always present, may be better perceived if sleep and glucose are in balance. It is always present, but the balance of life needs delicate tuning. The car has been serviced, and the engine is happy with the fluid digestion. But what about the body behind the steering wheel? The two must be alert, and several chocolate candy kisses will add quick energy.

Linus' blanket for warmth, and a nice pillow to comfort the brain waves. These are a blessing today.

Freedom empowered

Stretching every day with purpose and meaning. The clock continues to unwind but the soul ticks with enthusiasm. The direction isn't the GPS formula, but an intuitive unseen force that spells surprise!

The wash cycle and drier are all on timers. The day emerges. I clean; however, the steering of the intuitive can only be answered in quick little thought nudges.

Just thinking about the intuitive is not enough. Answering the urge to respond in action is required.

How? Through individual sensitivity to people, places and things. A wavelength of empowerment from the All Powerful One; the Eye and Ear of prayers sent, and hands and feet to respond. The unrestricted release of empowerment into the right place and time. Learning is solidified when verification arrives without a postage stamp.

86

Laughing is a healing joy of thoughtfulness. Recording the experience is like lighting a candle that suddenly flickers into an illumination of freedom. Why was this last word expressed? Only an author's question mark of wonder too!

Distractions and meditations

When temptation strikes, is it met head on or is it like stubbing a toe? Can temptation be something simple like feeling the need to put on a nice comfy bathrobe and climb back into bed?

The list of things to do can be plagued with should and shouldn't dos! The balance of life shouldn't be judged by others. Allow openness to rule.

The temptations of life are distracting, and dealing with these can be like searching for which smoke detector is blipping. There are those so self-contained that only prying off the covers with a screw driver can halt the alarm. No smoke in the house, only a burning desire within the soul to make right decisions. Searching through the hide-and-seek of life can bring moments requiring loneliness. Creative reaching for a book of faith can prepare for the next step. Is there a perfect timing that regulates action?

The purple robe and pen are resting, and silent reading begins. Joy! Don't deny your own self-expression waiting for others' input. Turn on the day with sunshine, and even shadows will disappear.

High noon of course!

Purpose

"Purpose" is an elusive word shrouded in the mist of life. Do you allow purpose to snooze in the dormancy of the seasons? Wondering about purpose or seeking it could be a thought urge flickering like a candle.

Indulge in this instant that can break through silence and become the restless spirit. Know the direction of your hidden talent. This is personal and individual.

The exposing of "self" entails a willingness to be vulnerable. Purpose thrives as the potential of expression, a gift to be shared. This inner surprise package is as colorful as a box of crayons or the opening of a paint tube. Every potential has a unique signature.

The promise of joy is ignited into being and shared with others. Don't deny purpose!

Outburst

Words suddenly begin to pour forth like blessings visibly given. Hello, power steering, with that touch of the heavenly hand!

The plants have nodded their heads from neglect of water while family needs were met. In mid-afternoon their colorful heads were bowed. Quickly the hose was turned on, and refreshment was given. Only seconds after turning off the faucet and returning to the screen door waiting to close, large heavenly drops arrived from a skyward cloud, and an unexpected afternoon shower deposited grace. The forest was shrouded in this lovely rain and mist. Five minutes of surprise and the rain clouds passed, and sunshine emitted light again. Thankful prayers of recognition that the showers of joy had blessed land, flowers and my recognition. There's no doubt that power steering exists in many forms to prove that the Garden of Life, thought, and existence are tangible. Power steering inspires awe and sharing.

"Thank You Lord."

An autumn seed of thought planted and waiting for growth and self- discovery.

Running the race

Power Steering can carry you past the
crossroads where temptation interrupts your
direction and purpose. The race, like a marathon,
can be won, or it can be lost due to hesitation. The
urge to stop and give no more effort can be a strong
impelling force. That's when following your own
intuitive GPS is so vital. The inner will must have
the strength and courage to move ahead. This is
advice having to be followed when the easy way
could be chosen.

Food for thought!

Advice penned when this has been experienced
and rewards still unknown. Take the challenge and
continue the race. An inner calm has been restored
by not questioning the decision made.

Getting a break

Surprises like just a little wish that previous
commitments had been made a month in advance.
Awake at 3:00 a.m. and up at 4:00 a.m., quite in
need to cancel those two appointments. But
crossroads were successfully passed and continuing
on. First appointment met even though difficult.
Okay, here comes the second, and nausea just can't
rule supreme. So peanut butter was an antidote, and

instead of leaving early to do several errands, just stopping at the sofa as a rest stop.

Watching the time just a few more moments to linger. Then the phone rang, it could have been a missed call, but it was the luncheon guest saying she would be a bit late. She had to wait for a repairman for her washing machine. "Would you like to cancel and make it another day?" came this driver's question. She thought for a moment, that would be alright because she needed to go to "Urgent Care" to get her leg wound rewrapped. No joking, the conversation flowed to a get-together later.

Returning to the sofa rest stop was such a relief and proved that power steering can truly be tangibly felt. Little instants in living on the very edge of faith without requesting. Amazing!

A popular word, love!

A thought emerged from reading a book this afternoon, and there wasn't any mention of love. It was only implied. Was it ever retained or ever found?

A gentle touch of the pen reaches for inward wisdom. It may flow forth or just be lost in emptiness. An unseen moment reaching for expression. If there is time? Is there love? Does anyone know the matching answer? It can't be found in being pushed across the threshold of a chapel and a waiting ceremony.

The harmony of oneness lost without any reservations among the no vacancy signs. The time moved right into the highway vehicle and raced past the romanticism seen in a distant view. The turn of the highway of life demanding schedules to meet and oneness lost in an emptiness of desire.

A distant surge of generations of the Old World gripping youth's learning that emotions shared weren't to be made visible. Reckless decision, and the beginning of a wrecking crew. Darkness with no honey in the moon. Every year begins with First Night – was there ever this in the human wedded moorings? Outspoken questions never verbal in openness or even now? Waves of memory must be gently closed for another day of opening the window. Put away these attic thoughts! Cold coffee will do for now.

Oh that's right it's Sunday!

Catching Joy

Do you ever just sit quietly waiting for inspiration to awaken?

Is the soothing flow permeating your being into potential action? The course has only a new day to find expression. The phone hasn't rung, and the bed hasn't been made as yet. What tangent might disturb this waiting power?

Close the eyes, and listen to silence, strong and reassuring, that life is still within veins of blood and thought. Smile as the stomach cries, "Too much coffee this morning!" A sign of moving back and forward between the veils of existence.

No page yet to turn except in anticipation and excitement to be shared somewhere out there. Change a word or two, but even the editing doesn't become criticism. However, the editing can cause a broken bridge to be rebuilt. A large unlit blue candle just patiently sitting beside an Indian vase. Each lighting thought without any hurricane raging at sea. Smile and think, "The author has freedom of expression, and happiness does peak, swell and rest on a shore." This silent ignition is your own key to turn on. Choice! Decision! Joy!

Oh my! Power Steering just jumped into gear. Walking to the door, and there the sunlight had just woken the beautiful miniature snapdragons. Run for the camera and catch this instant of perfect lighting. Joy caught on film!

Patience

Reaching for a light switch to receive light. Reaching for wisdom and insight requires action by the individual. A simple thirst requiring a quench in the throat can lead to the strength to find your way through life's little or big deserts. Breath of hope infuses the soul to pour forth peaceful strength.

Stop to question how? Only you and your heavenly parent can know or recognize the answer!

Close the earth-given eyes, and wait for soul's merging insights. There's no rumbling of the body in resistance. A peace of the metamorphic butterfly. This symbol means developing strength and freedom to fly when the time has reached out in anticipation.

Life has its little signals, and the thermometer of change can be overwhelming. Be still and wait for the energy of patience to click into action. The endowment of patience from the restlessness of

94

worry is a quiet gift of understanding in itself. A tiny punctuation mark can mark the completion of this growth moment.

Rejecting the instruments of expression makes an empty fountain. It takes just a pen to return to the everyday portions of expression, which can be granted with appreciation.

Meandering

A silent inner clock awakens awareness. The
eyes flicker without thought, and wakefulness
becomes opportunity. The unseen causes this
mystery to take place only after a few hours of
sleep. Does thought stimulate the mind and move
into the being of expression? The complexity of
gifts is waiting to emerge! Wrapping thoughts in the
comfort of quiet, and enjoying the warmth like that
in an old bathrobe. Life continuously moves like a
river trickling into wider view. Following its
meandering adventure into pathways dawning.
Reaching for the hurdle to pour forth a new
substance called truth!

Castles still standing on far away shores hold
mystery. They await appreciative eyes of awe.
Wonder and intrigue are little touches of a new spell
arising. Soft fragrances may have a lingering of an
old tobacco pipe in the library, and just a tiny
perfume remaining against a coverlet. Sensitivity to
the past enriches the present and births a calm that
inspires and refreshes the hidden soul.

The rush of schedules of people leaving. Sound
interrupts our stillness, and again the clock takes
precedence each day. Perhaps the early morning or
the late night opens a little window to catch a new
dimension. Hello, quiet thought! You are a

discovery of another new world. Not searched for, just suddenly the happening of joy and pleasure of a now written memory. *Meandering gone!*

Grab on!

Grab hold of power steering before it races away. The joy of feeling the autumn warmth to lift to another level. The feeling of inspiration reaching beyond the library door into the Writer's Group. It's the wave lengths of the unknown with so much space to grow. The leaves outside are softly spinning before the crinkle of the autumn floor.

The joy of a lecture the night before set the stage for today. Looking past a seatmate's ear to the visual screen wasn't a distraction at all. Critiquing, like the rhythm of a writer's pen, must not lose the strength of words. It matters not if the words are in place, out of place, or beyond imagination. Writing is a captured enthusiasm that releases joy just like the seasons of now. The 'to be' is meant to let the windows and doors to be open to the flow of happiness heart. Power Steering is a powerful energy that is here to be shared, or it is your choice to let it disappear. Deep breaths to envision a river scene, to traverse the mind of soul and say, "surprise!"

97

Midnight calling

The modern intuitive hasn't gone to sleep in the after-midnight hour. It nudges the body to move along with the feet to get paper and pen. "But I'm tired and I'm going to close my eyes." "Oh all right, but you'll miss the blending and time lost to opportunity." "What opportunity?" As eyelids begin to droop, there's a tiny smile that removes the creases of the lips. "You forget to mention the unique opportunity to share, you are your neighbor's keeper at times."

So back when the grocery cart had been filled with essentials, I was steering along the back of the store to check from curiosity that the 93% lean meat might be here. Then, at a cold storage meat section, stood a little lady with dark hair. She was bending to touch the display. The 93% lean was there, and this writer mentioned that to the lady that the meat was very good. Showing her with fingers touching the neatly wrapped roll how to cut and make perfect hamburgers, I said, "Oh, and it makes great spaghetti." My comments were a help to her. She hadn't been able to read the labels.

"Oh, I'll get some!" she told me.

For me, just a nice feeling of helping a stranger. In packing the car trunk there was a little voice, "Oh thank you so much!" The little dark haired lady was hurrying toward her waiting husband. So interesting to remember this incident in the still of the night. Ordinary, and yet a memory captured forever.

Lifting storms

The sounds of the night waves crash against the shore. A rhythm untarnished by human touch. Storm of yesterday left with such a profound imprint upon sky and memory. As the surf continued to tumble, and break against the shore, a portrait was building in the sky.

A voice called out, "come and see," to share with family a building rainbow of soft colors, becoming brighter too! The hues turned vivid, and suddenly a companion building rainbow became the stronghold for the white arching bridge high above.

The beginning and end of the rainbow with a powerful steering shape right in front of our eyes. The beautiful sky and moment resting each on the Atlantic current. Leaving this breathless view, the western sunset was creating its own evening promise too.

The unsurpassed beauty of each, all within minutes of discovery. Blessings holding sway to today, tomorrow and on. "Thank you for sharing these awesome moments for memories capsule." Treasures by the sea. Outer Banks, North Carolina.

Power steering returns

Don't cry over spilled potato flakes on the counter. These just seemed to have multiplied after dinner last evening. It doesn't take a snow blower to remove, so that's an autumn blessing.

The doors are open, and the screens are doing their own thing. The breezes are free to enter one and depart the other. Another blessing: the lack of hurricanes this season. The washing machine can continue its revolutions, and soon a quiet calm pervades, except for the old camping-stove coffee pot, which is still perking away.

Okay, little odd segments of morning, but noticing the little things becomes the balm of healing. The puffing steam of the coffee pot leaves a fragrance that seems to keep good company with time.

The spirit of abandonment free from the design of worry has a soothing texture too!

Power Steering is like the cloud-hidden sun that later breaks out into full rays of wonder.

It has its own direction, but so often it is just misjudged like, "Maybe not now." But it forges ahead. Direction of purpose can come from an unexplained source.

100

Time on the Turn

Power Steering returns after silence and time racing on in a mystery of discovery.

Road maps aren't always as fluid as memories cascading into a new reality. Suddenly, in an open box of little treasures, was a picture loved and rediscovered: A picture holding a book of promise and a smile always cherished.

Holiday joy bundled among letters of precious friends, and all of their cherished families gathering together. Gifts of their taking time to share. Such an awesome 'joy' that's hard to define, each a touch of God's miracle of this season of gifting and sharing. It's truly, "Time On the Turn."

Dear Lord, guide me through these vast fields of uncertainty. It's the growing winter of barren trees and silent grasses. Words seem pitiful in expression, and the sunrise of joyfulness hopefully will soon arrive. Distant fingers of day are reaching the solar heights, and vision will soon erase the cloud of fog and see with clarity.

The denseness of the night is now gone, and pathways of choice lead to the decision for Joy. Only a fallen poinsettia petal remains.

"Thank You Lord for Now."

101

Birth

In silence not a solitary thought is trickling
through. Yet the urge is rising to meet the unknown.
A distant thermometer is indicating that the heating
unit is about to perform. Warmth is acting as an
incubation for nurturing of new life. Perfection is a
product of heaven's hand, reaching out to provide a
new blessing. The miracle of birth. It's a New Year
about to be born into freshness and beauty. How it
is shared will be the awesome power of steering a
new course.

A thought almost denied, and a discovery made
of life, love and happiness.

A new Year's Resolution to be Joyful and
Happy!

Being Led

Power Steering has many roads to choose, but
the most delicate is the thought path. Being led by
this thread of discovery into the intuitive. It's a
golden invisible thread like a little web caught in a
sun ray. The instrument of *how* can be equally
surprising. A PBS program with a great speaker on
three kinds of love: Human, Spiritual and Divine.
The stop of night brought rest, and from another
source came the spiritual journeys of distant

102

cultures, all woven into an expression of divine love.

In the evening of time, I had a feeling of having lost connection. A seldom-used wireless phone produced an e-mail that otherwise would have been lost. The thread of love has traveled great distances through the Divine Grace and mysterious power on High. Yes, Power Steering, you can't be put down, and we have more miles to travel.

A sudden realization that no longer a classroom to teach in, but a whole world to share by teaching from the tip of a pen. A thought that I will include in a New Year's Resolution to be "Joyful & Happy".

Small steps

Power Steering has a tendency to spring surprises. It has a fragile nature that is as delicate as an unannounced snowflake. No jolts, just a little feeling of changing direction.

Problem solving can be like a mountain with hairpin curves, or it can lay out like a little prayer map, and let resolutions arrive in due time.

A sudden thought can be an inspiration that needs to be put into action. Race not with the odometer, but in a microsecond make a decision. It's that element of making a decision within the

103

intuitive of Power Steering that suddenly produces a wave length of joy.

Measurements are not necessary. By faith these snowflakes bear fruition upon their translation into water. Time not to be tapped out like musical notes by hands. No, the hands just let love, and they let go under the direction of power steering.

Eagles of freedom

The flight of a treetop bird became a surge of question. I wonder what it is sitting on, so high on a thin branch? A moment of wonder became a prelude of delight. A distant sight of sunlight on its turning head. There's a crown of white, and then in flight its white shawl gleamed in the nanosecond of departure. A young eagle! Free flight and a sight for my breakfast table delight. Soar on and the day has begun.

The rescue

Welcome to the world of little thoughts. Shall we say that my near-death experience was averted by the intuitive moment of my dear son-in-law? He had planned to leave his studio and go to the basement train room. But he just happened to look out the front window, and he saw a familiar object lying in the driveway. Ice on the stony surface had embraced the shoes, and the loss of my power steering took charge. Unable to move, couldn't even slide. He said those four minutes of sheer terror could have been frozen in time. The Lord blessed me to be rescued.

Inner strength

Inner strength of being draws from a question.
"Where shall we go this afternoon, Lord"? Hunger
pangs began a list of what restaurant might lure my
writers craving! "One, too noisy," Two, too far!"
Next the need for a cozy environment where alone,
self would feel that circumstance. "Aha…a little far,
but why not drive out toward the river road and
rediscover an old-fashioned little motel restaurant?
    It was busy, but not too busy to find a little
table for me. Sitting in my little haven of old-
fashioned country goodness. The menu drew all-
stars' award for two ham biscuits and red bliss
potato salad. Soft music of somewhere back in time
allows weaving words to record the now. Looking
beyond the passion of words in the lyrics for the
ears, while the eyes were drawn down past the lace
curtains on to the greening patio. "As time goes
by," words that seem to fit.
    Someone looking toward my nook of peace,
and being tantalized by the orange cup of coffee.
It's hard to close this book of sentimental moments,
reaching out toward others.
    A relaxing calm courses through my pulsing
veins. I find sharing again.
    Afternoon shadows drawing little impressions
on the outside leaves, and bringing an

106

understanding of polka-dotted sunbeams. The dining room has emptied, and it is time to pay the check for such a priceless place to return again and again.

"Carrot Tree, I love you!"

Blessings

The Lord's blessings…as these never sleep.
Blossoming beyond the shorelines of continents and
into the realms of space. Words fail to carry
gratitude into the Holy of Holies. Only the essence
of joy can reach these heights.

If you have never experienced this unseen
elation, then know that the joy is the Holy Grail of
all blessings.

This cocktail of wonder and contentment
produces peace. The healing.

Mind, hand and soul connected. Woven into
life's heartbeat.

"Thank you, Lord!"

Acknowledgements

The abundant encouragement of family and friends makes the acknowledgements another page in capsuled memory. Trying not to forget the individual help begins with a young woman who initially said, "You've got to publish", and *Journey into Fulfilment* became a tangible shared joy. As Cathy Leach picked up the excitement, she too began her own mission as a writer and soon-to-be published author. My mentors include the interest and introduction to our Williamsburg Writers Group by Daniel Wetta, author and publisher. The multiplied encouragement brought Chesapeake Bay Writers Group into sharing.

The discovery of Xulon Christian Publishing Company has provided blessings of encouragement and counsel for publishing and marketing, *Journey into Fulfillment* and *Time On the Turn*.

My pen name was created from Scottish ancestors many years ago when conflict of interest was raised in my being a teacher and writer. The happiness of M. J. Scott will continue as new books are already in the wings. There's *Enthusiasm* waiting to burst on to the printed line. And, perhaps, poetry lines caught along the highways of life. "To

109

be continued" would whet the inspiration for a comedy of experiences.

Join the ranks of writers with everyone having a story to tell, and sharing becomes another adventure!

M. J. Scott, USA, 2016

About the Author

M.J. Scott is the author's pen name. This is one that she is enjoying with a flourish of happy publications. Writing is truly a given expression that everyone has within and can, with time, be nurtured into discovery. As a teacher and photographer, M. J. has attempted to capture this intuitive gift of awareness. She lives in a beautiful English colonial town that has a wealth of author residents. Her life-long journey is blessed with a B.S. in Education and M.A. in Mass Communications.

"Creativity is our laboratory
Love is our lamp...
Youth is our energy...
Hello, world!
Hello, out there
Stars in space!"

M. J. Scott, USA, 2016